AMERICAN ASH

AMERICAN ASH

Poems by Michael Simms

RAGGED SKY PRESS
PRINCETON, NEW JERSEY

Published by Ragged Sky Press
270 Griggs Drive, Princeton, NJ 08540
www.raggedsky.com

Library of Congress Control Number: 2020939743
ISBN: 978-1-933974-39-2

Text and cover design by Jean Foos

Front cover art is a detail from a photo by Sara Van Note. It shows the scarring from tunnels made by the emerald ash borer. The invasive insects have infested and killed millions of ash trees in North America.

Photograph of author: Eva-Maria Simms

This book has been composed in FF Scala and Neue Haas Unica Pro

Printed on acid-free paper ∞

Printed in the United States of America

First Edition

for Eva, Nicholas, and Lea

Contents

Three

One

Hammer

On West Carson Street, skinny white boys
Slump in front of tattoo parlors
Scratching their arms. Girls
In short skirts take long pulls
On cigs, stand in groups
Smiling at the men who drive by
Hungry and shy...*the realm*
Of the hungry ghosts the Buddha
Calls it. I don't know anything
About anything. But I once saw
A guy hit another guy
Over the head with a chair
And a cop with thick wrists
Put handcuffs on the brawler
And haul him off. And I saw
The bartender stomp the broken chair
And throw the sticks
In a dumpster in the alley
Where a junkie was shooting
Heaven in his tattoos.

My son wasn't any of these guys.
He was the carpenter in the bedroom
Of an empty house down the street
Nailing a one by four to a two by four
Reinforcing a stud in a wall
That's seen better days.
His long fingers hold the nails
And he swings the hammer
From his shoulder for more force.

My son was born blue. His shoulders
Were so wide, he got caught on the slide
Into the light. Or maybe
His long dark hair got caught
In the instrument listening

To his heart. Or maybe
He just didn't want to start
This long difficult walk
To oblivion. But whatever
The reason, I know he was stuck
In the birth canal and when
He came into the light
The midwife massaged his chest
Until he gasped. And now, when I look
At his beautiful hands
Which can drive a four-inch nail
Into a board with two whacks,
I think of his tiny hands
Twenty-seven years ago,
Opening and closing
As he took his first breath.

I don't know anything about Jesus
But I'm happy my son
Doesn't live on the street anymore.
Walking down Carson Street
I saw a beaten down boy
Begging for spare change,
But it wasn't my son. I saw
A young man hand a small bag
Through a darkened car window
And the slim hand of a woman
Pass cash to him,
But he wasn't my son. I don't know
Anything about Hell, but I've seen
A junkie sitting on the sidewalk
His knees pulled to his chin
Staring at nothing—just the feet
Of people walking by,
Trying hard not to look at him.

The Summer You Learned to Swim

The summer you learned to swim
Was the summer I learned to be at peace with myself.
In May you were afraid to put your face in the water
But by August, I was standing in the pool once more
When you dove in, then retreated to the wall saying
You forgot to say Sugar! So I said *Come on Sugar, you can do it*
And you pushed off and swam to me and held on
Laughing, your hair stuck to your cheeks—
You hiccupped with joy and swam off again.

And I dove in too, trying new things.
I tried not giving advice. I tried waking early to pray. I tried
Not rising in anger. Watching you I grew stronger—
Your courage washed away my fear.

All day I worked hard thinking of you.
In the evening I walked the long hill home.
You were at the top, waving your small arms,
Pittering down the slope to me and I lifted you high
So high to the moon. That summer all the world
Was soul and water, light glancing off peaks.
You learned the turtle, the cannonball, the froggy, and the flutter
And I learned to stand and wait for you to swim to me.

for Lea

Hands

Every man who works with his hands
Has seen that look. Perhaps we showed up
To patch the roof, service the furnace,
Or unclog the sewer, and the pasty
Bank manager expounds his idiotic theory
Of what should be done. His wife
With her $200 haircut points her
Manicured finger at the wet place
On the ceiling. We do the work
And stand there, not knowing what to do
With our hands as she makes out the check
Complaining of the cost. As we explain
What was involved, she looks at us
As if we were just released from prison,
Correct in her questions, rude
In her attitude. Her husband brags
How he could've done the work
But doesn't have time these days
Busy with clients, blah blah blah.
They despise us because they depend on us.
How long will they survive in the coming collapse
Of their roofs, their pink bathrooms
Filling with shit, their Wedgewood china
Traded for scraps of food?
After they've burned the last stick
Of furniture in the fireplace
They'll flee their useless homes,
Beg to join us beside the fire,
Greedily devour our rabbit meat,
The bowl of weeds our wives gathered,
Admire our hairy large-knuckled hands,
And tremble as we howl with the dogs at the moon.

for Nicholas

Oh Darlin'

I like it when women I don't know
Call me *Darlin'*. There's something
Kind and generous in the tone

Without being sexual. The intimacy
Of strangers is luminous, the way
We wish well for the man who lost

His car keys, the woman coming in
Out of the rain, the girl who missed
Her bus, the boy who stutters.

The waitress who offers more coffee
Calls all the men at my table *Darlin'*.
She may be somebody's wife,

Somebody's mother, somebody's
Friend, but right now, to us
She's the intimate stranger

Named Dolores, which means sadness,
Inviting us with a smile to have dessert.
You want me to alamode that
For you, Darlin'?

Love

When I was a child, my mother told me
God has many faces
And She reveals Herself

In many ways. God might be
The cleaning lady who came
To our house on Tuesdays,

Or the woman in rags sitting on the sidewalk,
Or the blind girl lost in the bus station.

You never know, she said, who She is
Or what She has in mind for us.

     *

This from a Southern Baptist girl
Whose family sent her sisters to college
And passed her by. She learned

About the world through novels
And movies—endless stories folded

Into endless laundry. She bore
Five children in five years.

This kind generous woman
Overwhelmed by work,
Sustained by dreaming, blinded
By the bright light

Of love, raised denial
To an art form. Everyone she knew
Was a secret perfection.

Our best selves were exactly
What she knew us to be.

Her husband was not
A narcissistic bully,
Vain, egotistical, and angry, no,

He was a hero who charged
Into work every single day
To provide for his growing and
Perfect family. Her sister was not

A lesbian who hid a 40-year
Relationship with her partner,
Living a necessary lie,

But rather a woman who so loved
Her friend she would risk
The insults and injuries
Of bigotry.

And I...
I was not a lost young man
Baffled by life, who drank too much,

But her shining prince,
Her Byron, her Cary Grant.

*

When she shared her vision
Of God's many faces
With her brother-in-law,

The pastor, he slammed
His fist on his desk
And proclaimed, *Blasphemy!*

She never spoke of it again.
But once, I saw her sitting on the sofa
Stroking the cat, pausing at a page

In *National Geographic*—an illustration
Of Kali, the blue four-armed goddess,

Tasking her many children,
Nurturing, disciplining the unruly
World. The Divine Mother,

Her long pink tongue sticking out
Defiantly, stands with one foot
Stolidly on the ground,

And one foot on her husband
Shiva, the Destroyer of Worlds,
Who seems oddly content lying there,

While she, the Mother of Time,
Holds the dark severed head
Of his enemy in one hand, another hand
Holding a bowl to catch the dripping blood.

Wolf Corner

I thought your death would change everything
But the Brazos River has not changed its course,
And the shrug of these brown hills,
The jagged indifferent line of mesquite against the horizon,
The strings of spittle hanging from the mouths of cattle
As they chew cud in the narrow shade of the water tower
Remain as I remember

Although Wolf Corner, where we rode our bicycles
To see the rotting carcasses of coyotes, wolves, and wild dogs
Nailed on the wooden scaffold as trophies—
A custom, I'm told, ranchers adopted from the Comanche
Who hung scalps on a tree as a warning to our great-grandfathers—
Is now the entrance to a shopping mall.
Walmart and KFC glisten in the Texas sunlight.
In a dirt island in the middle of the asphalt,
A small cactus garden blooms.

Our ancestors, the Irish and Cherokee who settled this land,
Horse-breakers, carpenters, farmers, builders of towns,
Comanche fighters, freeholders, despisers of lawyers and politicians,
Are still here. Their bones are beneath the soil.

for Elizabeth Ann Simms Yeary (1957–2007)

Muse

As a musician, he was solid and reliable, but unimaginative. His chief talent lay in being in the right band. He enjoyed drinking and taking drugs, still in the initial phase of an addiction that would later ruin him. But for now, he was a young musician in a college town, so he had his choice of beautiful young women.

His attraction to the old woman surprised him. The bar was closing. The other musicians had packed their gear and stepped out for a smoke before going home, and there she was, sitting on a bar stool, looking at him. She had long white hair, a thin wiry body, and steel-rimmed glasses that almost hid the bright blue eyes that seemed to be seeing him more clearly than he was used to being seen.

They went back to her place, a small house on the edge of town. At the doorway, they kissed, moved to the bedroom, and fumbled with each other's clothes. But she suddenly stopped, removed his hand from her half-open blouse, and shook her head. She said she was sorry, but she couldn't go through with it. She thought she could, but that time of her life when she could make love with a stranger had passed. She hoped that he wouldn't be angry, and she wouldn't blame him if he left, but she'd like for him to stay the night, and in the morning, she would make him breakfast.

He was relieved. He had had far too much to drink and wasn't sure whether he could rise to the occasion. They talked for a while, and he fell asleep.

The next morning, he woke in a wide bed alone. Out the window, he could see a scrim of shadow cast on the bright snow by tree branches. Beyond the small fenced yard, a cornfield with broken stalks, and in the distance a house with smoke rising against a blue sky. The bedroom was tidy and sparse with a surprising lack of the dolls, stuffed animals, and cute knickknacks he was used to seeing in young women's bedrooms. He got dressed and walked into the kitchen where she stood at the stove, her back to him.

Years later, he would remember her like this—her long white hair falling down her back, the floral robe, the soft blue slippers, the smell of bacon and coffee. The kitchen was small and neat with copper pans hanging on the cedar walls. The floor was made of unfinished planks worn smooth. He put his arms around her, and she leaned her head back against his shoulder.

Many times through the years, he remembered the woman. The memory became smooth and fixed, like a stone he would pull out and hold in his hand to comfort him. He played in hundreds of bars and clubs. Although he never got much better at the guitar, and never learned another instrument, he became more versatile, able to do a credible job at a Polish wedding or a rock and roll school reunion. He played in a country-western band off and on for a few years, wearing a wide-brimmed Stetson. He eventually let go of his fantasy of having a big hit, and just tried to get through each gig without embarrassing himself, sipping beer and saving the hard stuff for later. And when the club was closing, he often looked over at the bar, half-expecting her to be sitting there, looking at him as if she'd known him forever.

Scarf

Yesterday I was standing at the corner of Carson and 19th in the Southside waiting for the light to change. To my right, a young man in a Pittsburgh Steelers cap crossed the street, pulling a pair of gloves out of his jacket when a scarf fell out of his pocket into the middle of the street. Not realizing he had dropped it, he kept walking. I called to him, *Sir! Sir! You dropped something!* But he didn't hear me and kept walking. A middle-aged blonde woman on the opposite corner looked at me wondering what I was yelling about and I said *He dropped his scarf!* And pointed. She turned toward the young man who was already twenty yards down the block and yelled at him, but he didn't hear her; however, an old African American man noticed her and yelled at the young man who kept walking on, oblivious to the chain of alarm behind him. Trying to get his attention, I yelled *Black Hat! Black Hat!* And the blonde woman and the old man picked up the cry *Black Hat! Black Hat!* and the young man turned. The old man pointed at the blonde woman and she signaled the young man to come back to the corner. Which he did—he started walking back, puzzled. The blonde woman held up her hand to stop the traffic, walked into the street, picked up the scarf, and returned it to the young man who smiled, turned and continued on his way. I have no idea whether the scarf was important to the young man, or whether he would have missed it at all, but it was a moving experience for me to be cooperating in this small gesture of kindness. The old man and the blonde woman smiled and waved at me, and I felt a surge of gratitude to be among such decent people in this lovely city in a dark time when the light of kindness seems so rare.

Black Brick, Yellow Brick

I will die in Pittsburgh on a beautiful day,
A day, I imagine, much like today.
I will die in Pittsburgh. Don't turn away—
It will be a Monday, like today, in Spring.

Yes, it will be Monday because
This poem arrives on a Monday
With its rhymes all awry
And never so much as today
Have I felt so alive.

Michael Simms is dead. They beat him
Because he was guilty and also,
As you know, he was innocent.
They held him in quarantine
And beat him hard with questionnaires

And with taxes. The witnesses
Are the beautiful Mondays,
The radiant Tuesdays,
The Wednesdays that belong
To someone else in another town.

after César Vallejo

A Story about My Daughter's Kindness

When Lea was living in Botswana, she once met a man on the road holding a kitten. He told her that he was going to have to drown the kitten if no one would adopt it. Lea, being a kind person who loves animals, said that she would certainly adopt the kitten. The man said it would cost her five pulas. But, Lea said, if you don't want the kitten, why would you insist on being paid? Because my family is hungry, the man said. Lea paid the five pulas and took the kitten home.

A few days later, a woman with wild eyes showed up at her door with a goat. She said that she would have to kill the goat unless Lea paid her twenty pulas. Lea said I'm not going to pay you twenty pulas for a goat I don't even want. The woman took a small knife out of her apron pocket and held the blade to the goat's throat. Do you want to be responsible? What's twenty pulas to you? You are a rich American and this is just a poor Botswana goat. Have you no heart? Lea, being a kind person who loves animals and also being a brave person who right now was a little afraid of this woman with the wild eyes, paid the twenty pulas and took the goat.

Lea named the kitten Masa, and she named the goat Bantlé. Masa was happy in the house, and Bantlé was happy in the yard, and Lea was happy she had saved both their lives.

A few days later, there was a ruckus at her front gate. She looked out the window and saw half a dozen people, each with an animal. There was a man holding a very old, very sick rooster, a woman with a mangy dog, and four children each holding an animal—a green lizard, a sleeping mouse, an orange bird wearing a blue hat, and an animal that looked like a marmot, or what Lea thought a marmot might look like if it wore a ribbon around its neck and yawned incessantly. On the other hand, maybe it was a sloth. Wait a minute, there are no marmots or sloths in Africa. Well, whatever this creature was, Lea didn't want to own it.

Lea realized she had made a mistake in buying the kitten—and a bigger mistake in buying the goat. She wasn't about to compound these mistakes by buying the menagerie outside her gate. Obviously, word had gotten out that the American would pay cash for animals.

Lea was afraid she would have to buy every animal in the village, and then people would start bringing animals from the countryside. She had to put a stop to this.

Meanwhile more people were gathering in front of her house. They didn't have animals; they just wanted to see what she would do. Her paying money to crazy poor people so a kitten wouldn't die and a goat wouldn't die was the most interesting thing that had happened in the village in months. Of course, everyone loves a kitten. But a goat? People milked goats, or they ate them, but they didn't try to save them from their fate.

Lea went out to the gate and told the people that she would pay one pula for each animal they brought, but today was the last day she would be buying animals. She gave a pula to each person, petted each animal, and then asked the person to take the animal home because she had no more room in her house.

And no one brought her another animal during the rest of her stay in the village.

As for Masa, she became a pretty good mouser. And Bantlé spent the rest of his life in Lea's yard, happily munching the weeds and bushes.

The Marriage-Bed

The marriage-bed is the center of happiness,
    a point from which all things ripple outward,
    a nest from which all things learn to fly.
It is the sign of return, part of the great rhythm
    of the seasons and of the years.
It is the dream of return, the strength and faith
    that sing of home.
It is the wren's nest woven of twigs and string,
    the swallow's nest of saliva and mud.
It is what we return to, as migratory birds
    passing over marshes and fields
    dream of the end of the journey.
It is what frightens night-devils away,
    even in winter.
It is the tree that grows through the house,
    the hollow of the tree that has never known death.
It is the crystal of all feeling, the flower of all
    understanding, the small containing the large.
It is the nautilus growing its many chambers of love.
It is the sudden outburst of one who has long been silent.
It is the idea that a calla lily can be shaped
    like a wineglass on a long green stem.
It is the heart-stone.
It is the name of all names
    that thinks it is a star and a rose.
It is a conch-shell rough on the outside,
    pearly in its intimacy.
It is a snail rolling over and over
    building a staircase.
It is an animal, an almond, a repose.
It is an oyster opening in the full of the moon.

It is a mouth telling a secret.
It is a kiln where clay battles fire.
It is the simple happiness of sleeping on a boat.
These are the walls we've pressed back into a circle
       in the shape of our merged bodies
And it will take a long time for the waves
       spreading from the center of our intimacy
       to reach the ends of the world.

for Eva

Evening

Always it will be late summer in your mind:
Birches give off a full and dark light

With a motion you know will abide and return
Every evening. You are changed

By small things: an elm seed spins
To earth, and like your talent for the cello

The possibilities remain enclosed.
Being ordinary makes you a hero—

Sweeping the porch, looking at the sky,
You become more than yourself. The solace for being

Dull is being perfectly at ease with the world.
All afternoon

The afternoon sails in and out the window,
And the first star starts the lake singing.

Going Deaf

Now is the time for drowsy tanagers. —E.S.

First I lost the tick of snowflakes hitting glass.
Then the sound of the cat's tongue running over her fur.
It used to be I could almost hear her tail moving,
The muscles of the back stretching, the yawn going to a different register...
I lost the buzz of the fly, the distant hammer of my neighbor fixing his roof,
The whine of wind in the rafters and the exact words you speak
As you walk away, rooms opening to other rooms, houses full
Of music I'll never hear as I walk by. The tinny laughter
Of television sitcoms I don't miss,
Nor bus-farts nor gunshots of the cops
But Louis Armstrong, Bessie Smith...missing a few notes
Means losing the whole song, the way all the beads
Fall to the floor when the string breaks.

What I miss most are the sounds you wanted me to hear:
The *too-weet, too-weet,* of the hungry towhee,
The *sisisisphree* of the chickadee, the *twonk–twonk* of the woodpecker,
The red-tailed hawk as it cries to its mate,
Your mother singing, and through the years her voice cracking
And shattering and coming to rest inside you.

I do see the flash of the cardinal in the branches,
Even the wood thrush almost invisible in its nest of leaves,
The silent song sparrow carrying yarn in its beak,
The return of hundreds of crows to our mountain every evening.

For a long time, you thought I didn't have a hearing problem,
But a listening problem. And damn it, you were right.
So many sounds I ignored when I had the chance to hear them.
Every morning a riot of song, the stars going out, one by one—
I could almost hear them.
Every day our children learning to speak,
Every afternoon leaning into ourselves.
What's the sound of two hands clapping?

Lost are the double entendre of the bed squeaking at night,
The slant rhyme of wind in the trees,
The anapest of crickets. *Basso profundo* of the bullfrog.
All that remains are the bright light on the snow
And the wind moving the last leaves on the poplar.

Soon comes silence, first the small silence of the deaf,
Then the Big Silence growing from a spot of darkness
Becoming a shadow under a tree and finally night, starless and forever.
Perhaps as my hearing fades, my listening will improve,
So every sound will call us home
Like our mothers in the evening.
Every fear becomes a sound like
Echoes in the pool hall—

Perhaps I will hear Chopin as I take off your bra.
Remember when we were first married,
How we loved being lonely together,
Riding the slow train from New York to Pittsburgh,
The rhythm a sympathetic magic between us?
Back home, we lay in bed, kissing like waterfalls.

Music will become a dream,
Then a memory of a dream,
Then nothing at all, just a word,
An unformed idea
Like color to a blind person
Or the smell of hyacinths lingering
After they've been carried out of the room.

You, my best half, know
When I hate myself, I hate us
And you flee to the woods to be
With your birds, your snow-filled trails,
Your deep ravines and wooden bridges,
Braided waterfalls, stone culverts,
And the singing of the stars
As they go out one by one.

Robin, the sentinel bird, lets out a cry
And the pileated woodpecker chases the hawk away.
Oh love, let us ride the lonely train to Pittsburgh forever
Where the November symphony grows fainter every year.

Four Poems Tracing an Arc of Forgiveness with Real World Examples

My Brother Who Is Dying of Cancer

My brother who is dying of cancer
Tells me the time has come
To forgive our father because
It's not about us, it was never about us
Only about the children entrusted to us
To praise, to nurture, to protect.
He says he learned this lesson
From our father who failed
At the task so thoroughly.

A Few Weeks before My Sister Died

A few weeks before my sister died
She called me, and we had a long talk,
Joking and ribbing the way we used to do
Before our estrangement. My anger
And her pride, or perhaps her anger
And my pride, had done us in,
And it was so wonderful to hear
The old Beth. I didn't know at the time
That after years of drugs and drink
And therapy, she had given up,
And her call to me was her way
Of saying goodbye. Our last words
To each other were *I love you.*
A final act of kindness to me
Before she blew her brains out
In a bathroom in Llano, Texas.

I Was So Sick of Myself

I was so sick of myself
Tired of everything tainted with myself.
When I looked at a flower I saw
Only myself looking at a flower.
Sky, trees, birds, streams,
Children, houses, streets, cars,
Work, play...I knew it all
Because it was all myself.

In the airport, I saw crowds, everyone traveling
Home to me, talking on their phones as they walked,
And I heard them speaking of my own self-absorption.
When I listened to the news, it was news of me, of how I
Am changed by the comings and goings of laws and officials.
The only war was the war within me.
The only hunger was the gnawing for something more.
The only death that mattered was my own.
I saw my own torn body among the war-flung dead.
I was God and the Creation.
When I kissed the woman who loved me, I was kissing myself.
It was all me, all the time.

And then...and then...my shell
Grown too heavy with nothing to support it,
I collapsed into myself like a dying star,
I became a black hole that nothing escaped from.
I sat and stared, sat and stared,
Not eating, only a sip of water now and then,
Barely breathing, as all the images of my life flowed through my mind,
Beside the window I felt, rather than saw,
The light come and go, come and go,
As afternoon faded to evening, night to day.
In the dying half-light of my 63rd year, I saw
My father's fists, my mother's exhaustion, my grandmother
Whipping my naked little brother,
His screams from the next room.
I saw me being raped in a bathroom

By an older boy when I was eight,
Drinking, drugs, anger, desolation
Blew through me and came to rest
And I woke from my trance, knowing
I had crossed into another world.

In the hour before sunrise, I reached across the bed
And touched the arm of the woman I've lain beside
Ten thousand nights, and she was she and I was I
And I could love her without thinking of myself.
We took Josie for a walk in the streets of our neighborhood.
Late April and pear trees were dropping their white petals,
And Josie had to stop to sniff each small thing,
Dog turd, dropped ice cream cone, garbage can,
And Eva kept the leash loose and easy and let the dog lead us
Into the alley where the dogs, her friends,
Were barking, and a small girl came over to us
To pet our puppy, and life was good, and there were no decisions to make
Or things to think about, life was all about the snow
Of flowers and the yip of a puppy and a child's small hand stroking fur.

Welcome Happy Morning

Comfort from the summer garden and the winter roof
In the garden the weathervane shifts above
The greenhouse our son built in the backyard
In the winter the Monongahela flows beneath the ice
Until finally we ask God for nothing but death
Won't you sing to me once more
All along the road
Weave me a wreath of white roses
The radiant days with you, the tender nights

Two

American Ash

The Veteran

Beside the barn a huge stack
Of logs cut and split with imperfect
Symmetry and Howard his
Bald head like a bullet is
In his undershirt

           Marine tattoos
On his bulging biceps and I
Remember things he's told me
About the Nam and the drugs
And living on the street and finally

Meeting Suzanne who loved him
Whole again. They moved here
To raise horses which healed him
Until Suzanne passed from cancer
And he wept in my arms like a baby
And started drinking again

Invasive Species

Howard says *Back up your truck*
We'll load er up
Ash? I ask
Having seen the stumps
Beside the road
Yeah he says
You know it's against the law
To haul firewood cross
County lines don't you but
It don't matter no more
With ash wood
They're all dead now anyways

Emerald ash borers
Howard says
They come from Asia about
Thirty years ago and now
They pretty much killed every ash
In the east a shame he says

I offer to pay him for the firewood
But he ignores me and we load
Half a ton in the back of my truck
And stand there a minute or two
Resting and I think

They must have looked
Like old men, the ash trees
Dry and gray and brittle
Death spreading from one tree
To another down the road

Abandoned Tractor

Howard is looking at his forty
Acre spread where he grew
Corn and soy and horses
It's mostly scrub now

He kept the mule
That reminds him of him
And a few of the horses
Too old to sell

He hasn't the heart
To kill them

The soil he and Suzanne worked
Is fallow, choked
With weeds and the smell
Of failure

Gasoline

Old warriors rarely
Say anything about
People they killed or
Horrors they saw instead
They talk about the fun stuff
Of war the killer weed and
The mama-san they spent
A weekend with

        Or maybe
The strange feeling of stepping
Off the plane in Dulles
Having misplaced their lives
And now living someone else's

Once when he was drinking
Howard told me how he watched
Seventeen Vietnamese children
Mistakenly machine-gunned

By our own choppers and Howard
And his buddies were ordered
To pile the bodies
Pour gasoline over them
And light them on fire

And I thought Holy Jesus
These men we send to do
Unspeakable crimes
In our name

Bury that shit real deep
Where no one can ever find it

Tree of Life

When the young man wearing a yarmulke
Asks *Excuse me sir are you Jewish?*
I want to say *Yes*
I've studied history and know
Something about suffering
But that's not what he means.
He's trying to find ten men
For a minyan
At Rodef Shalom down the street

And when the young man carrying a Bible
Asks *Have you heard the Good News?*
I want to say *Yes!*
The cherry trees are blossoming!
And when he asks *Have you been saved?*
I want to say *Yes!*
I've been saved by poetry
From a childhood of abuse
And humiliation—
That's a kind of miracle
Isn't it?

But I know
He wants to know
Whether I've accepted Jesus
Into my heart and there's the rub
Because my heart is so small
And Jesus is so big

When I walk into a cathedral
My heart sings, when I walk
Into a forest the trees sing
And when I walk down the street
The legless man on the sidewalk
Puts his whole heart into the ukulele
Oh Susanna we are saved

It is springtime in Pittsburgh
And in America

My friend Rashid is an atheist
Because his mother was killed by a bomb.
His father died unhappy and his sister
Has moved to Australia. Rashid blames
All his tragedies on religion
And he may be right.
We all have our tragedies
And maybe God is to blame.
What do I know?

Well, I know this much:
Anyone who has grown a garden, raised a child
Or looked at the sky far from a city
Knows the truth. So, yes, I'm a believer
In the Big Dark, the Ur-unknown,
The sense that my little mind
Is part of the Big Mind
I'll never know

But I have to say
God, like a lazy cop,
Never seems to be around
When you need Him

Somewhere a soldier is beating a boy
For throwing stones. Somewhere
A priest is raping a child.
Somewhere a girl in a marketplace
Has a bomb strapped to her chest.

My friend and her mother
Were in the Tree of Life synagogue
When a man who hated immigrants
Pushed through the door of their faith
With an automatic rifle. You know the rest.

for Arlene Weiner and Philip Terman

Uncorrected Proof

My mother who was much wiser
Than I knew used to say
Make sure there are mistakes
In everything you do
So the gods won't be jealous

And sure enough
I find my mistakes spreading
Like bluebonnets
On the dry plain beside
The Llano River

Where we spread her ashes
With the ashes of my father
Whom she loved

She loved this imperfect man
And found beauty
In his mistakes
Imagine

And the river carried her ashes
Down to the Brazos
And the Gulf of Mexico
And who knew
She'd come back as a breeze
On this patio

*

It is springtime in the hill country
And the bluebonnets are like a blanket
On the dry land

And the Indian paintbrushes
Dab their reds and yellows

As the shadow of the storm
Passes over them

*

I once knew a composer
Who listened so intently
When I spoke
He didn't hear me

The grief passed long ago
And what's left is
Sunlight and shadow taking turns

In the morning the storm builds
In the afternoon the rain passes

*

A translator famous for his versions
Of Akhmatova
Said he was trapped
Between heaven and earth
Imagine being so in love
The mistakes we make
Keep us on the ground
Imperfect and happy

Which was it?
Rain falling on dry sand
Steam rising in the valley
The mountain turning blue
In the gathering dark?

Or was it
Rosy fingered silence

As my friend Jose says
Yes, metaphors are

Things with sharp edges
That can hurt you

*

Most days I'm sleepwalking
Passing trees without seeing them
Hearing birds and neighbors
Who want nothing more
Than acknowledgment a simple
Good morning or a nod

And then as if as if
For the first time ever
I'm awake this doesn't happen often
Just every now and then like
Sunlight on a patio with bougainvillea

A profusion of hibiscus and a scent
Of salt carried by a breeze
From the ocean hundreds of miles away

My Old Man Can Whip Your Old Man

If we did not fight, were not greedy,
did not demand anything, were not selfish,
and did not want to benefit ourselves,
we would have no anger.

— *Venerable Hsuan Hua*

Ed Asner

As for me, I'm not much of a fighter. A couple of dustups in high school left me chastened. But my old man once beat up Ed Asner, or so the story goes.

In 1949, Dad and his buddies were in a bar drinking with Asner, a short muscular son of an ironmonger in south Chicago. Asner had heard of my dad because he'd punched out a racist marine for insulting his friend, a Nigerian exchange student, and Asner, who'd been a navy signalman in the war, claimed he'd never met an infantryman he couldn't whip. When he looked at Harry Bill Simms, what he saw was a skinny kid with thick glasses, but what he didn't know was that this skinny kid had boxed as a flyweight in the Army and competed in the Golden Gloves tournaments in high school, and he knew how to handle himself.

They exchanged words, and Asner knocked over the table and came at him swinging. My dad jabbed him in the jaw with his left, gut-punched him with his right, then kicked him in the balls. My dad and his buddies left the bar, as he used to say, before things started to get regrettable.

Years later, the *Mary Tyler Moore Show* would open with the fluffy song and the credits. Ed Asner's scowling face would appear on the screen, and my dad, now a successful attorney, would say, "I beat that guy's ass thirty years ago in a bar in Chicago. He wasn't so tough. He bragged about being a signalman. Can you believe it?"

Don't Fuck with Poets

I remember the Leather Balls Saloon on Greenville Avenue in Dallas where Jack Myers, pugilist-poet, bartended with a sarcastic attitude appropriate for the clientele—workmen, bikers, prostitutes, and even frat-boys who were laughed at and told to go home.

One night a drunken plumber had been riding Jack all evening until finally Jack cut him off, refusing to serve him any more alcohol. The plumber called Jack a "pansy-assed poet, prolly a fag."

Jack had had enough for one night and quietly asked the guy if he wanted to step outside and settle this. The two went out the back door with six of us following, wanting to see the fight.

Jack didn't hesitate. He walked quickly to the plumber, tripped him, sat on his chest, grabbed him by the ears, banged his head twice on the asphalt, and yelled

DON'T FUCK WITH POETS!

Hippolyta

And today I'm at the Y, swimming laps in the blue pool of memory, so to speak, thinking of my dad and Jack Myers, and other men I've known and how we get all tangled up in our pride like Achilles and Agamemnon who hated each other and whose hatreds made them immortal.

I towel off in the locker room and watch the guy I call Hercules, who's a vegan, scowling at sly Odysseus, attorney of record for the frackers, who's explaining how a little poison won't hurt the school children, considering how many jobs are at stake. Odysseus is jabbing his finger in Hercules' chest. As my dad would've said, I leave before things start to get regrettable.

On my way out, I pass through the gym where Castor and Pollux are shooting hoops, talking trash, and Hippolyta Queen of the Amazons is training for the ring. A tall black woman shining with sweat, legs like tree trunks and fists like hammers, she's pounding the padded hands of her trainer who's knocked back with each punch. Hippolyta and her magnificent body are one.

On the wall behind her, a hard pine board is burned with the single word VALOR. She knows training gives her strength, speed, endurance. Anger is for amateurs.

Swamp Thing

I wanted to tell you
How I grew up outside Houston, the edge
Of the suburbs, wandering the woods

And bayous, following the railroad tracks
Deep into the sugar cane fields, but I kept thinking
Of Swamp Thing, a monster,

An amalgam of mud and water lilies,
Vines and cattails, a dripping thing
In human shape living in the swamp,

Protecting plants and animals,
And I was remembering the deep woods
Of oak and sycamore where pools of water

Were alive with frogs and minnows,
And how if you stood still long enough
The frogs sang *om* like an army

Of Buddhists and one
Sweltering afternoon I watched
Two older boys with a net seining

A pond and pulling out fish and
Netting a turtle which they beat
With sticks until the shell

Cracked and the naked turtle writhed
And the sun dried its flesh, a wanton
Unspeakable crime. And I went home

To read my comic book
Swamp Thing in which Dr. Anton Arcane
And his nightmarish Army

Of Un-Men sought the evil ones
Who murdered his wife, and in the middle
Of the night my father caught me

With a flashlight under the covers,
And said we had to talk, and he
Accused me of talking back to my mother

And when his fist hit my belly
I felt it sink deep all the way
To my spine, and when he pulled it out

I thought I heard a sucking noise
Like a boot pulled from mud,
And I knew he could no longer hurt me.

       *

The next morning I rode my bicycle to
Wolf Corner where coyotes and dogs were
Hung on a wooden rack to discourage coyotes

From stealing calves, and the story was
That Comanche hung scalps
There to scare the whites, but

The whites came anyway and stayed
And my Irish-Cherokee ancestors
Ranched there, and later

I lay in the dark and thought
Of the snapping turtle the boys killed,
How it could take off a finger, and

An alligator gar, a monster
Left over from the dinosaurs,
Could rend flesh if you

Weren't careful, but it wasn't violent.
It was almost tender. To show me
It didn't hurt, he did it to himself,

Slipping the table knife
Into his anus. I was eight.
He was the older boy next door.

He was my best friend and all
I knew of love. Afterwards
I went into the woods alone

And sat on a log beside the bayou,
Watching the water slow
With mud and rotting vegetation,

Deer coming to the water's
Edge early in the morning,
The possums and foxes, the wild dogs

That lived in the woods, free
From the leash and chain-link fence.
I imagined myself a swamp thing,

Guarding trees and animals.
But over the next few years, the trees
Were toppled and burned

In huge bonfires, and Scarlett O'Hara
Mansions and Roy Rogers haciendas
And Frank Lloyd Wright knockoffs

Rose in obscene excess, the stream
Channeled through cement pipes
To invisibly carry sewage underground.

     *

I mourned the trees,
The possums, the gars, and the turtles.
I lay in the dark defiantly reading

With my flashlight under the covers
Of Swamp Thing, one of the Elementals
Born when a being dies in flames

And merges with the Earth,
The Elementals became protectors
Of plants and animals throughout history,

Eventually joining the Parliament of Trees,
A group mind of former Elementals.
Over time the membership grew with beings

Such as Eyam—a trilobite,
Swamp Knucker—a dragon,
Bog Venus—a medicine woman,

Ghost Hiding in the Rushes—
A 3rd-century Chinese sorcerer,
And of course, me, Swamp Thing

—An early 20th-century scientist.
Until recently, the Parliament
Was stationed in a grove

In Brazil, south of the Tefé River,
While our minds dwelled
In the realm of the Green.

And lying in the dark, with
My anus bleeding, throbbing in pain,
I imagined myself one

Of the elementals, able to
Transcend pain and defend
The children. And once

United with the Parliament
Of Stones, we set out to destroy
Humankind for their sins against

The Earth. We had to fight off
The fungus-based Grey,
Invaders from another world

Who preached peace while
Actually helping humans with
Their lies. Our allies were

The heavenly power called
THE WORD which passed on
All their power to Swamp Thing,

Me, who refused in the last
Second, giving humanity another
Chance, a few good people,

Mothers and children who
Survived the massacre at
The hands of THE WORD.

And the Parliament of Trees
Is now eternally burning
In the realm of the Green.

Who Will Tell Them?

It turns out you can kill the earth,
Crack it open like an egg.
It turns out you can murder the sea,
Poison your own children
Without even thinking about it.

Goodbye passenger pigeon, once
So numerous men threw nets over trees
And fed you to pigs. Goodbye
Cuckoo who lays eggs
In the nests of strangers.

Goodbye elephant bird
Who frightened Sinbad.
Goodbye wigeon,
Curlew, lapwing, crake.
Goodbye Mascarene coot.
Sorry we never had a chance to meet.

Who knew you could wipe out
Everything? Who knew
You could crack the earth open
Like an egg? Who knew
The endless ocean
Was so small?

Right now, there are children playing on the shore.
There are children lying in hospital beds.
There are children trusting us.
Who will tell them what we've done?

Who's the Rat Sister Linda?

Who's the rat Sister Linda
Is it perhaps the lawyer
Who works for Justice
Or the priest who drinks
In the cloister or the housewife
Who hates her husband
Or maybe it's me
The drunken young poet
Staggering in the footsteps
Of Charles Bukowski no
It is Frank Varelli who broke
Into your apartment to find
Evidence you're a terrorist
And then tried to seduce you
To get sex on tape
To blackmail you into informing
On your friends in the sanctuary
Movement but one thing
Frank didn't expect to find
Was all you wanted was
Peace and justice the way
Thomas Merton and Dorothy
Day and Dr. King and
Joni and Mel and Ziller
Want the world
Safer and kinder and our
Own government as it turns
Out is the terrorist organization
Not the barber locked in
Guantánamo or the nun
Tied to the back of a jeep
Dragged down the road
Taken into a field and raped
Again and again by the soldiers
Nor is it the man who brings
His daughter to the mission

And says she's been violated
By soldiers and the poor girl
Can't speak and the father
Clenches and unclenches
His impotent hands.

The Informer

Frank Varelli as we
Found out later walked into
The Dallas FBI office
On a Friday afternoon in
Spring 1981 wanting to
Be an informer because his
Father was a Salvadoran
Army officer fighting
Communism and Frank
Wanted to help his country
Be free but free only for
People who looked like him
Not all those dirty little
Indio peasants scraping
A life out of tiny plots
Of maize and beans
Who could barely speak
Spanish because Frank was
An educated man who
Lived in the US and wore
New blue jeans and a plaid
Shirt and tried to look like
One of us leftists who
Hated what our country
Was doing/had done to
Brown people starting
God knows when perhaps
When Columbus landed
In the islands and kidnapped
Native girls raped them and

Took them back to Spain as
Specimens for Queen Isabella
To inspect at her leisure

The Assassination

I often think of Óscar Romero
Shot while giving mass at
The Church of the Divine
Providence and wonder
Who was the gunman
Who dared to kill an archbishop
Delivering sacraments to
The poor and why kill this
Man who was a conservative
Who condemned poverty
And torture and rape and
Who believed in God
The way the rest of us believe
In rain and I wonder
Was the gunman a true
Believer in his cause or was
He just a hired assassin of
The corrupt oligarchy and
What other crimes had he
Committed in the name of
The greater crime of enslaving
A nation and why is my
Country tis of thee always
On the wrong side of history?

A Brief History of Blowtorch Bob

In 1932 a donkey was worth
More than a campesino so
The people rose up and
Demanded and the oligarchs

Sent in soldiers who slaughtered
30,000 people and arrested
The leaders and cut off their
Hands and raped their wives
And daughters and in 1944
University students brought down
The government but couldn't
Hold on to power and after
The student massacre of 1975
Civil war broke out lasting
12 years with the US on the side
Of the oligarchs calling the leftist guerillas
Terrorists but it was Death Squads
Trained at the School of the Americas
Who massacred mourners at
The Óscar Romero funeral
And committed the Sumpul River massacre
In 1980 and the 1981 El Mozote massacre
And the 1982 El Calabozo massacre
Followed by the Tenango massacre of 1983
And the Guasilinga massacre of 1984
And 27 other massacres of civilians
During the 1980s carried out
By American-trained soldiers
And through all this blood
The US gave millions to
The oligarchs who hired
Men like Roberto
D'Aubuisson also known
As Blowtorch Bob
For his favorite tool
Of torture

Say the Names

Let us say the names
Of the martyrs
Maura Clarke

Dorothy Kazel
Ita Ford
Jean Donovan
Dragged behind a jeep
Beaten raped murdered
By Salvadoran guardsmen
Who were convicted
With their sergeant and
Went to prison but
The generals who ordered
The atrocity never
Faced justice
So let us say
Their names as well
Carlos Vides Casanova
Head of the National Guard
José Guillermo García
Minister of Defense
May they burn in Hell
As for Frank Varelli who
Befriended us only
To betray us I feel
Only pity and as for
Sister Linda she sued
The FBI for violating
The rights of citizens
To speak out for what
They believe and the
FBI settled out of court
A big pile of money
Rather than be embarrassed
In the public eye and
I've heard that Sister Linda
Used the money to
Help refugees flee north
And find safety in
Canada and so I say
Fight on Sister
Fight on

What Holds Us Together Keeps Us Apart

Dragon's Blood

I dream of a forest in heaven
Thick stands of American Ash
American Chestnut American Elm
Saint Helena Olive and of course
The Great Sequoia

And on a nearby island
Dragon's Blood Trees
Oozing red resin
Cinnabar
Which tinted the violins
Of Stradivarius

The Fabric

The loss of each species
Diminishes us
Tears at the fabric and
The news is too much
With us

The bees in their
Hives are dying the manatee
Sliced by a motor blade
Bleeding in the shallow
Cove where her kind
Have lived since we
Were human the forests
Of Amazonia are burning

We are burning
We are dying

Shoes

Something there is
In the American heart
That wants to destroy
Everything beautiful

The dirty child at our border
Who walked 500 miles
Sharing a pair of shoes
With her brother

And we
Have no pity we have no shame
We refuse love and how
Could we how could we want
Something different than
Love?

Driving Home

Afraid of Covid I went
To the East End Co-op and talked
With Jackson who helped me find
White mulberry bark dong qui root
Skullcap and stinging nettle
And stopped by the produce aisle
To pick up broccoli sprouts
And Midnight Express and
Carried my environmentally
Correct burlap bag with vegan
Hippie stuff to the checkout
Where I praised Jackson
To Melissa his boss and went
Outside got in my hybrid
And drove down Penn Avenue
To Dallas Avenue and cut past
The universities and across
The Liberty Bridge and up the
Long hill glancing at the river
And the blue city turned
Right then left pulled
Into the driveway and looked up
At the window where Eva is
Writing this morning after a long
Talk over coffee about whether
She is good enough to write her
Book about poverty and trauma
And violence and gave a small prayer
Of thanks and wow and sorry
To be so lucky so full of joy
In these last days before
The whole thing collapses.

Three

If you are meditating and a devil appears, make the devil meditate too. —George Gurdjieff

Antbed

You may remember my father
Died when I was eight
My mother closed up
The house and we went to stay
With my grandmother for a few months

I wasn't fully aware of my father's death
I was quite happy that summer
Aunts and uncles felt sorry for me
Treated me kindly I was given a puppy
The two of us roamed
Freely the country-side

When my mother and I returned
To our house and this
Is the point of my story
There was an antbed one and a half
Feet high two feet wide
In the middle of our living room

The ants who must have sensed
The house was unoccupied
By humans had carried the dirt
Grain by grain from the yard
Through the cracks between the floorboards
And across the thick-piled carpet
To build a spectacular pyramid
A temple to the puritanical gods
Of organization and blind work

I got down on my knees
And watched a line of the black insects
Struggling toward the city of their making
Each worker carrying a tiny pebble
Or a bit of food a butterfly wing
Or a breadcrumb one little guy

Was shoving a moth a hundred times
His size across the top
Of the pile of carpet a feat
I imagine akin to a man
Maneuvering a downed Lear jet
Across the top of a rainforest

Three inches away a line of workers
Empty-handed so to speak
Marched in the opposite direction
On a parallel highway my admiration
For these civilized insects
Was immense their city must have taken
Ten generations to build

I imagined the intricate and sublime
Architecture labyrinthine passages
Winding down to a golden chamber
Where the giant queen sat
In her magnificent perpetual
Pregnancy attended
By telepathic nurses who knew
The shifting temperature of her moods

While I was roaming the fields
Around my grandmother's house unaware
Of time passing an entire civilization
With poetry heroes and commerce
Had risen in the shadow of our china-cabinet

My mother was less impressed
With the civilization that had sprung up
In our living room she immediately called
An exterminator I burst into tears
As white-suited men shoveled away
The antbed poisoning the inhabitants
I imagined the screams of the victims
As they watched their homes crumbling
Their young dying

With the antbed cleared away
And the carpet restored to its original
Sterility I felt
My father's death for the first time
He would not be coming through the door
With a baseball glove or an atlas
As a gift to make up for his absence

He would not be sitting in his easy chair
Reading the newspaper asking my opinion
On world events considering
My answers carefully he was not
In the garage fixing the toaster-oven
Or in the yard pruning the apple tree
Or in the kitchen gently teasing my mother
Out of her anger I would not ever again
Be visiting him in the hospital

On Saturday we brought flowers
To his grave and I tried
With all my inconsequential strength
To straighten the gravestone which always
Seemed to lean toward the north
Into the wind and storm and snow

Why I Didn't Tell

At seventeen
My sister was kidnapped
By her ex-boyfriend
And sold to his friends

Who kept her in a cage
So they could rape her
At their convenience

They finally let her go
They would kill her
If she told anyone

So she didn't
And I didn't

I didn't know
About the abuse
Until twenty years later

When she told me
It didn't seem real
It was too large and strange
For me to hold it

Like being handed
A demon barely restrained
On a leash

Right now
I'm sitting in a circle
Listening to friends
Whose last names
I'll never learn
Talk about recovery

The drag queen who
Finally feels pretty
Damn fantastic
Offstage

The carpenter whose house
Is falling down
As he speaks

The ex-mafioso who
Was raped by a priest
When he was eight
And who knew nothing
But hatred
Until this morning
When he fell to his knees

My sister drifted through
This program like a ghost
A few days a few months
Of being clean
Always returning
To the release of drugs

Freedom and peace
Not being anyone
Floating through a cloud
Of unfeeling

I've not told anyone
Of the horror
She went through
The pain of keeping
Secrets that eat
You alive

What is my pain
Next to hers
Cutting her arm

Repeatedly not wanting
To feel then feeling

Finally
She shot herself
With a .22 pistol
She'd hidden
In the bathroom

Our parents were sitting
On the front porch
Behind a curtain
Of denial

Didn't hear the gunshot
Were barely aware
She was in the house

But I don't blame them
They too
Had been handed
A demon barely restrained
On a leash

Heart of Glass

In Herzog's great visual opera
The hero stands on a cliff
Above a valley where a river
Of molten glass carries
Light to the sea

And everyone who watches
The film thinks yes
This is how it is the heart
Is broken then melted
And the feelings flow like

Molten glass I thought
My wife having recently
Left me every touch
Was like sandpaper
On my raw skin

Because I had been
By everyone's account
A total ass never mind
Cassandra let bygones be
The beginning of new

Bygones and did I mention
I was a total ass in
The film the hero is
A seer who has been
Called down from the hills

And he says the factory
Producing the ruby red
Glass will burn down
And with it the secret
Of producing the glass

And the Baron there's
Always a baron in fairy

Tales isn't there the Baron
Believes the glass
Has magical properties and

The secret is lost and
The Baron and the whole
Damn town descend
Into madness which
Reminded me of

My own madness after
She left I sat on
The kitchen floor all
Night drinking and the
Next morning I got up

Went outside walked
Through what must have
Been a beautiful April
Day with birdsong and

Light I didn't see
Coming down
Through the leaves

The Garden and the Drone

We come to the garden because it is beautiful.
Arborvitae, hydrangea, anemone—
Even the names are beautiful.

The men who call themselves our leaders
Seem far away. We feel free to be kind,
To walk from here down the street,

Greeting our neighbors, stopping to give
A dollar to a ragged man sitting on the sidewalk.
Beauty wants us to be kind.

Can we believe in kindness the way we believe in rain?
Can we practice kindness until it becomes a habit,
A custom, a ritual of small acts?

If we step over the homeless man
On the sidewalk, then we can easily ignore
The child in Syria blown apart by our taxes

And our drone hovering over the garden
Where the wedding party waits
For the bride. A missile is launched

And everyone dies.
But such cruelty seems far away.
Here in the garden where virtue is easy

We avoid the cold calculus of blame.
Arborvitae, hydrangea, anemone
Beneath the wide August sky.

Angela Fell in Love with Her Monkeys

Angela fell in love with her monkeys
In the lab and then she was ordered
To euthanize them and there
Was no choice she thought
Because they'd lived in cages
All their lives and her saying this
Made me think of Winchester
Our big black Lab who was
Calm and sweet and eager
To please the household
Except when fireworks erupted
Over the city and the noise and
Excitement drove him nuts and
He would escape the house
And run down the street past
The crowds looking up
At the sky saying *ahhhhhh*
Every time a flower of light
Filled the sky and Winchester
Terrified must have thought
The stars were exploding the moon
Was falling and he would run
For miles but somehow always
Found his way to Bernie's
Front porch to hide until
The sky was silent and
Hearing about Angela's monkeys
And thinking of Winchester
Barking at the bursting sky
Reminded me of Moondog
The blind Viking of 6th Avenue
Busking his records when few
Knew he was a brilliant composer
Self-trained by reading
Scores in Braille and living in
Manhattan when he met Charlie

Parker and liked the sense of
Humor in Charlie's music and
Donned a horned helmet so he
Wouldn't be confused with Christ
Having rejected Christianity at
An early age and instead posted
Himself near the 52nd Street strip
Where he christened himself
Moondog in honor of a hound
That used to howl at the moon
More than any dog
He knew and later he moved
To a house in Candor NY where
He maintained an altar to Thor
Who showed him the rhythms
Of city traffic and ocean waves
Babies crying and foghorns he
Loved it all and remembered
His father taking him to
An Arapaho Sun Dance where
He sat on the lap of Chief
Yellow Calf and played
A tom-tom made from
Buffalo skin and later he invented
Instruments such as
The *oo* and *ooo-y-tsu* and the
Hus and the *trimba* and he lived
The last 25 years of his singular life
With the Sommer family in
Westphalia not far from where
My wife grew up and he
Composed hundreds of compositions
In *snaketime* and *slithery rhythm*
And claimed *I'm not gonna die*
In 4/4 and he probably didn't
Because he sure didn't live
In 4/4 and I still hear his music
When I walk through the city and
Even Philip Glass said he learned

More from Moondog than
From Juilliard and I'm thinking
Of all this and Angela's poor monkeys
Living their lives in cages until
They're not needed anymore and
Winchester who ran for his life
From the sky unnaturally exploding
And I wonder what cage I live in
And under what sky.

Oh God She Says

Oh God she says
The dog has learned to spell
And suddenly the whole universe

Makes sense it's a living breathing
Cell with ribosomes and
Mitochondria and a tail and

Things hanging out of its mouth
Like spittle and we are lying beneath
The table waiting for food to drop

From the beings having dinner above
And we decipher meaning only if
It confirms what we already

Want as if nothing exists except
Our desire and nothing has permanence
Unless we see it today and tomorrow

We leave the room and the chair is still
There and I think of Feynman's marvelous
Universe this tremendous range of time

And space and different kinds of animals
And all the different planets and all these
Atoms with their motions are merely

A stage so God can watch human beings
Struggle for good and evil or if we want
A bigger stage because as Gracie Allen

Put it *never put a period where*
God has placed a comma we
Can demand answers

To the unanswerable and adopt
The uncertainty and
Embrace the mysteries we now

Experience so of course we
Are all agnostics but we can't stop
There we have to move

Toward understanding God
And embrace the true mysteries
Of the universe which are different

Than the mysteries which confounded
People thousands of years ago and
As Gracie says *I don't see what*

Difference it makes what side
Your bread is buttered because
I always eat both sides and so

I'm always uncertain of anything
Except the most basic answers as when
Josie learns T-R-E-A-T

Refers to her constant desire.

Our Father Who Art in Flowers

Our Father who art in flowers
In the corner of the birds/in the heart
Of compassion/in charity
In patience and forgiveness
Our Father who art in me
You are the One I love
The One who hurts me
The One who seeks the truth
Father of ours/you are the One
Who stayed with me
And the One who left me
Wounded by longing
Hallowed be Your name
For all that is beautiful
Good/fair/gracious
Lead us to Your kingdom
Of peace and justice
Faith and charity
Light and love
Forgive my mistakes
Forgive my heart when it turns cold
Forgive me as I forgive those
Who offend me/Forgive me
Even when my heart turns bitter
And troubled by ingratitude
Rid me of evil/of violence,
Rid me of pain/of heartache
And disappointment/But still,
When such difficulties are necessary
Give me strength and courage
To say Thank you Father
For this lesson.

Consider the Hummingbird

Consider the hummingbird
How like the mind it is
Flitting

Bee balm to daylily
1200 heartbeats per minute
200 wingbeats per second

In a universe 12 billion
Years old
In pursuit of love

The hummingbird can dive
60 miles per hour
In the courtship

Dance
250 breaths per minute
Forward backward

Its red throat
Is not pigment in the feathers
But a refraction

Of light like the shimmering
Of intelligence
We see

Everywhere in the garden

*

And the child (this would
Be me) at naptime
In kindergarten

Lying on a mat on the floor
In the darkened room
50 other kids

Miss Verlaine standing
High heels right next
To my head

Face up I silently slid my mat
Toward her feet until
My head

Was exactly between her high heels
And I looked up her
Nyloned

Legs looking up up up into
Darkness between
Her legs

Then slid my mat back
And pretended
To sleep

But little Alice Stuyvesant
Saw me and all afternoon
She looked

At me and I didn't know
Whether she would tell
The teacher

But I didn't care because I had looked
Into the darkness and
Survived

*

And looking up into the night sky
Is like that
The mystery is

You can't see much
But you imagine
Everything

Even God if you want to call it that
This intelligence, this
Cunt

This darkness we live inside and is
Everywhere even
Here

In the garden where the hummingbird
Moves from daylily
To bee balm

Its small feet tucked behind
Its muscled chest with more than
250 breaths

Per minute its wings beating 200 flaps
Per second its heart
The size

Of a peanut squeezing out 1200 beats
Per minute and how
Much faster

Is the mind with neurons sending electrons
Across 30 trillion
Synapses

Every second and how much faster
Than the mind is the mind of
The universe

Which as night comes we see
The stars and the stuff
Between

The stars
The living tissue
Of reality

That gives us this
Hummingbird

The whirring of its wings and the glint
Of red at its throat
A deep

Mystery in the mere fact
We experience
The world

As whole and beautiful with
color and music
and joy

In the redness of red the taste
Of mint the stars
Popping

Out like musical notes

The End of Civilization as We Know It

Roommate

I want to apologize for walking in
When the dog was licking
Your bald head as you lay
On the couch drinking rum
Straight from the bottle because
Your girlfriend called you something
You won't say out loud because
It's too disgusting you said without
A hint of self-pity just a whimsical
Smile that made me think of Einstein
Flunking math when he was younger
Than you with your strange sense
Of dignity considering the dog
Licking your bald head with big
Sloppy licks reminded me
Of a mop on a kitchen floor which
Also needs attention.

Neighbor

He says he's sorry for looking
In your window when the two of
You were tongue kissing and
Being shocked because you claimed
You were mother and daughter when
Really you were lovers and then
Suing you for painting your house
Top to bottom with the rainbow
Flag which was your coming out
To the neighborhood which started
A melee where a dog was shot and
No one wanted poor Rex to die
But this is what happens when

You live in a place where pickups
Come with gun racks and coyotes
Run down the street chasing cats.

Coyotes

When the coyotes surrounded you
They wanted to eat your dog not
You who called your boyfriend to drive
His pickup right into the middle of
The pack and scatter the coyotes
And you knew the coyotes were
In the abandoned country club because
Wolves and cougars were hunted out
A hundred years ago and the coyotes
Keep out the cats so the songbirds
Are everywhere spreading the seeds
Of wildflowers which carpet the old
Fairways and the ruined clubhouse
Where the owls live and maybe
We're okay with the end of civilization
As we know it.

Snow Camel

On Highway 80 near Sellersville
A camel was spotted in
The snow no one
Knows where it came from
But the locals have named her
Snow Camel and the radio
Said if you're missing
A camel please call the
Station to put in a claim
And somehow I don't think
This is odd because I know

What it is to be in the wrong
Life in the south I'm a northerner
In the north I'm a southerner
In the summer I long for snow
In the winter I long for sun
Somehow always looking
For a way out while also
Feeling right at home
Just about anywhere.

Road

You were being funny about your
Time in Vietnam telling about the time
You were riding in a truck and two
Women lifted their shirts and the driver
Slammed the brakes and the soldiers
Got out and took the women into
The field and fucked them and paid
Two dollars a fuck and then got back
In the truck and then you started
Crying and laughing at the same
Time crying and laughing and laughing
And crying and you couldn't stop and
Someone got you a glass of water
Which you spilled on your shirt and
Started hiccupping and we thought
Smoking a joint would help but
It didn't and later you said don't say
Thank you for your service instead say
We're so sorry we did this to you.

Suit

When you showed up in court
In a three-piece suit you'd worn

Only to weddings and stood in front
Of the judge he thought you were
A lawyer not the defendant and the
Other defendants showed up wearing
Orange suits and leg chains and
The judge asked where is your client
And you said I'm the defendant
Your Honor and he invented your
Defense and let you go to rehab
Instead of jail and when you got out
You bought a big bag of smack and
Stole money from your mother's
Purse and beat up your dealer
And made him pay your lawyer
And you were running a scam
On yourself only yourself yourself.

Bananas

Let's do something with the bananas
You said because they sit and sit
And turn black and no one wants
A black banana and it seems like
This is the way it is around here no
One wants to do what needs to be
Done only let things fail the lightbulbs
Burn out the roaches run around as
They please there's a rat that
Lives in the walls and we
Hear it at night dragging its tail
And the landlord wants the rent
And the light company wants and
The gas company and the water
Feels like it's coming up to my chin
I'm drowning in my own thoughts.

Drugs

You didn't choose drugs
Drugs chose you no matter
Where you hid them
They called your name
Whippersnatch Lossingput
Whirlymitch you were always
At a loss to know who you were
Or why things fell apart when
You touched them but never
You mind there's always
More confusion to fill
The hole inside you and
Now you've been clean and
Sober a few months and you
Want us to believe Attila the Hun
Has become Mister Rogers well
I don't think so.

Appliance

Now that we're middle class
I can't help but remember
The old collapses and how
My life was like an unplugged
Appliance taking up a lot of
Room with its expensive
Reminders of how things
Could be if only we knew how to
Turn it on but somehow it never
Happened instead we just thought
We were cool not to care but
We were just too incompetent
To be in charge of ourselves.

Snow

Getting old is like coming to the end
Of a novel you didn't like that much
But it's the only book you own
And you have nothing else to do
And the main character started out
As kind of an asshole and now he's
Less so most days but today he's an
Asshole again and you really don't like
Him but his wife is pretty cool except
For those few years in her early 50s
When she was in *meanopause* and
In this last chapter the snow is
Falling slowly covering the trees
And houses and everything is
Beautiful as you feel yourself
Floating over the city and you wish
The story didn't have to end.

Notes

"Tree of Life": On October 27, 2018, the Tree of Life Congregation in Pittsburgh was attacked during Shabbat morning services. The shooter killed eleven people and wounded six. It was the deadliest attack ever on the Jewish community in the United States.

"Who's the Rat Sister Linda?": On the morning of Saturday, February 15, 2020, I woke remembering my involvement many years before with the Dallas chapter of the Committee in Solidarity with the People of El Salvador (CISPES), a small group of anti-war activists who were concerned about the growing involvement by the U.S. government in the ongoing war in El Salvador. The leader of our chapter was Sister Linda Hajek who lived in Bethany House attached to Holy Cross Church in South Dallas, a poor neighborhood. The congregation of the church, which was almost entirely African American, had approved the use of the church as part of the sanctuary movement, a modern day underground railroad, which was taking hold among Christian churches across the country, and from 1981–1985, I was one of a number of people who helped Sister Linda illegally transport refugees from South Texas to Oklahoma, providing the Salvadorans with food, warm clothes, and small amounts of cash. During that period, it became clear that there was an informer tipping off the FBI. Through a process of elimination, Sister Linda deduced that the informer was Frank Varelli, a member of our chapter, who was working for the FBI as both informer and provocateur. Sister Linda filed suit against the FBI and, rumor has it, extracted a large settlement which she used to smuggle more refugees into the country. On remembering these events, I went online and read several articles about El Salvador to refresh my memory of the bloody history of the country and then wrote this series of five poems very quickly. I've decided to keep the poems in their original spontaneous form.

The events recounted in the sequence of poems are historically accurate, including the one that radicalized many Christians in Latin America and the United States: on December 2, 1980, four Catholic missionaries from the United States working in El Salvador were raped and murdered by five members of the El Salvador National Guard. They were Maryknoll Sisters Maura Clarke and Ita Ford, Ursuline Dorothy Kazel, and lay missionary Jean Donovan.

"Antbed": The voice of this poem and the memories it recounts are those of my cousin Michael George Ashie (1955–1997) who lost his father at a young age.

"The Garden and the Drone": According to an article by Tom Engelhardt published by *The Nation,* between 2001 and 2017 U.S. airstrikes wiped out a total of eight wedding parties in Iraq, Yemen, and Afghanistan.

This poem was commissioned by City of Asylum Pittsburgh to be read at the Alphabet City Garden on August 4, 2018.

"The End of Civilization as We Know It": This sequence of ten poems was created out of a challenge I gave myself to write a series of quick improvisations. Here were the rules: each poem tells a story in one sentence; each story recounts an odd or embarrassing incident that someone told me about recently or which I myself witnessed; and each story explores the theme "The End of Civilization as We Know It." A total of nine poems were written in less than an hour on November 29, 2019. Another poem, "Snow Camel," was written in a few minutes three days later and inserted into the sequence. I've decided to publish these poems in their first spontaneous form and not to revise them.

The last two lines of "Road" are borrowed from John Samuel Tieman's wonderful essay "Thank You for Your Service" about being a Vietnam war veteran—first published in Vox Populi. Tieman writes "Instead of 'Thank you for your service,' perhaps folks should say, 'I'm so sorry we did this to you.'"

Acknowledgments

The author is grateful to the editors of the following journals where versions of some of these poems first appeared: *5am, Mid-American Review, The Banyan Review, Connotations Press, Pittsburgh Post-Gazette, Pittsburgh Quarterly, Poetry, PoetryMagazine.com, Sampsonia Way, Telescope, Texas Observer, The Non-Conformist,* and *West Branch.*

Some of these poems appeared in *Nasty Women & Bad Hombres: A Poetry Anthology,* edited by Deena November and Nina Padolf (Lascaux Editions, 2017); in *Sheltering,* an anthology edited by Aileen Cassinetto (Paloma Press, 2020); and in three chapbooks published by Monkey Sea Editions, edited by Ziggy Edwards: *The Happiness of Animals* (2006), *Black Stone* (2010), and *The End of Civilization as We Know It* (2020).

Some of these poems were read by Garrison Keillor on the radio broadcast *The Writer's Almanac* (American Public Radio), and by the author on *Prosody* (WESA Pittsburgh) and on *The Karen Denard Show* (KERA Dallas).

"The Marriage-Bed" has been read as part of several wedding ceremonies and has appeared in church bulletins and newsletters in the American South.

"Evening" appeared in *Migration,* published by Breitenbush Books (1987).

Many of these poems were included in my blog *Note from the Editor,* published by Vox Populi (https://voxpopulisphere.com/).

A number of people have influenced me in the writing of these poems—far too many to name here. However, there are a few people who have been particularly important: Eva-Maria Simms, Naomi Shihab Nye, and Arlene Weiner. Also, I want to thank my editor at Ragged Sky, Ellen Foos.

Born and raised in Texas, **Michael Simms** has been active in politics and poetry for over 40 years as a writer, teacher, editor, and community activist. He is the founder of *Vox Populi,* an online forum for poetry, politics, and nature, as well as Autumn House Press, a nonprofit publisher of books of poetry, fiction, and nonfiction. He's also the author of four collections of poetry and a college textbook about poetry—and the lead editor of over 100 published books. Simms has won a number of awards and fellowships, including a Certificate of Recognition in 2011 from the Pennsylvania State Legislature for his contribution to the arts. Simms has an MFA from the University of Iowa and a Certificate in Plant-based Nutrition from Cornell University. He lives with his wife Eva in the historic Mount Washington neighborhood overlooking the city of Pittsburgh.